Runaround Rowdy

Story by Claire Saxby

Illustrations by Craig Smith

Dad slammed the tailgate of the truck shut. "That's it!" he said. "Rowdy has to go!"

"But Dad ..." said Paul, as he and the two dogs, Buddy and Rowdy, followed Dad across the yard.

"No buts, Paul. Rowdy's just no good at rounding up sheep, and we can't afford to feed animals that don't work."

Dad sat on the woodbox outside the backdoor, and pulled off his boots. Rowdy jumped up at him and barked.

Paul looked anxiously at his father. "Dad, I know he'll get the idea soon. Rowdy's only young. I'll teach him how to round up sheep. Please let him stay."

Dad sighed. "Okay, you can work with him for the rest of this month. But if Rowdy isn't any better—and I mean lots better—he'll have to go. I paid enough money for him. He should be a champion!"

He frowned and added, "We'll just have to get another pup. What a waste of money and time, having to start all over again! Buddy was never this much trouble."

Dad stomped into the house.

"Don't worry, Rowdy," said Paul, as he gave the dog a hug. "I know you can do it."

The next day after school, Paul took Rowdy out to the field where the sheep were. "Bring them in!" he called to Rowdy.

Paul pulled his arm back behind him, using the words and signals his father had taught him, but Rowdy wasn't interested. He just leaped all over Paul, barking and running around in circles.

"Look, Rowdy! Sheep!" shouted Paul. "You're supposed to push them to the end of the field and through the gate. Watch me!"

Paul ran around behind the sheep, waving his arms, and they trotted away from him and toward the open gate.

Suddenly, Rowdy overtook Paul and raced toward the sheep.

"Yes! Good boy, Rowdy!" smiled Paul. "That's it ... Oh, no!" Paul's smile turned upside down as Rowdy ran around to the front of the sheep and sent them back toward Paul.

Every afternoon, Paul practiced with
Rowdy. But although Rowdy was full of energy
and seemed to want to help, he kept running
in front of the sheep. This always sent them in
the wrong direction.

Paul wondered if Rowdy would ever learn
to round up sheep. There were only eight days
left until the end of the month!

He ruffled the dog's ears. "I've had
enough for tonight," he said. "Come on, Rowdy.
Let's go and get the eggs for Mom."

Paul walked through the vegetable garden and opened the gate that led to the hen yard. He stepped past the hens that were clucking around, and went into the hen house to check the nests.

He filled his T-shirt with eggs, came back out to the yard, and stopped. Where had all the hens gone?

"Oh no!" he groaned. "I must have left the gate open!"

He ran to the vegetable garden. "Rowdy!" he cried. "What are you doing?"

Rowdy was standing guard in front of the hens, which were huddled together in a corner of the vegetable garden. He had rounded them up when they had escaped! If one of the hens tried to move, he hustled it back with the others.

Paul stood inside the hen yard, and yelled, "Rowdy! Bring those hens back! What'll Mom say? You shouldn't even be in here."

Paul searched frantically for somewhere to put the eggs. But when he turned around, the hens were streaming back into the hen yard, fussing and clucking.

"That was excellent, Rowdy!" said Paul, with a sigh of relief. Rowdy's tail wagged furiously. "Now we'd better get out of here before Mom and Dad see you."

As Paul walked toward the house, he thought about the way Rowdy had rounded up the hens. "Rowdy brought the hens toward me," he said to himself. "And when he tried to round up the sheep, he brought them toward me, not the gate. Maybe I need to train him a different way?"

Paul put the eggs in the fridge and ran back outside. "Come on, Rowdy," he yelled. "Let's give it one more go!"

This time, Paul didn't try to get Rowdy to herd the sheep away from him. Instead, he stood near the gate. He was going to try to get Rowdy to bring the sheep **toward** him, just as he had done with the hens.

"Okay, Rowdy," he called. "Bring them in!"

Rowdy looked at Paul for a second, and then raced toward the sheep. He stopped halfway and looked back, but Paul just pointed at the sheep. Rowdy began to run again.

He went around behind the sheep, and began to bring them back toward Paul.

For the first time in weeks, Paul relaxed. Rowdy did know how to round up sheep, he just did it a different way from Buddy.

Paul practiced with Rowdy for a full week. Then, with one day to go before the deadline, they were ready.

13

The following evening, Paul and his father walked out to the field, with Rowdy bounding about in front of them.

"This had better be a good demonstration, Paul," said Dad.

"It will be, Dad," promised Paul.

When they got to the field, Paul headed toward the gate.

"You can't stand where the gate is," frowned Dad. "You must do everything properly!"

"Watch us, Dad," replied Paul.

He turned to Rowdy and said, "Bring them in, boy!"

Rowdy took off and, within minutes, he was moving the sheep toward the gate.

Paul stepped away, and Rowdy pushed the sheep through. Paul shut the gate behind the sheep and gave Rowdy a hug.

"Good boy, Rowdy, good boy!" he said, with a huge grin on his face. "See, Dad? He **can** do it."

"I can hardly believe it's the same dog," said Dad in amazement.

"Can he stay, Dad ... please?" begged Paul.

"Well ..." Dad paused, and Paul held his breath.

Dad reached down and patted Rowdy. "Okay," he said, "he can stay!"

"You can stay, Rowdy!" said Paul with a grin. He gave Rowdy a big hug, and whispered into his ear, "But you'd better stay away from the hens!"